NO
F*CKS
GIVEN

NO F*CKS GIVEN

"Naughty Words to Live By"

Sarah Knight

VORACIOUS

LITTLE, BROWN AND COMPANY

New York · Boston · London

Voracious / Little, Brown and Company
Hachette Book Group
1290 Avenue of the Americas
New York, NY 10104

littlebrown.com

First Edition: November 2022

Voracious is an imprint of Little, Brown and Company, a division
of Hachette Book Group, Inc. The Voracious name and logo are trademarks
of Hachette Book Group, Inc.

The publisher is not responsible for websites (or their content) that are not owned
by the publisher.

The Hachette Speakers Bureau provides a wide range of authors for speaking events.
To find out more, go to hachettespeakersbureau.com or call (866) 376-6591.

ISBN 9780316490856
LCCN 2022936433

Printing 1, 2022

LSC-C

Printed in the United States of America

NO
F*CKS
GIVEN

YOU NEED TO **STOP GIVING A FUCK** ABOUT WHAT OTHER PEOPLE THINK.

—THE LIFE-CHANGING MAGIC OF NOT GIVING A FUCK

Just because you're doing a ton of shit all day, every day, does NOT mean you have your shit together. More likely, it means you are **a high-functioning human to-do list** potentially on the verge of total mental and physical collapse.

—GET YOUR SHIT TOGETHER

UNLESS YOU'RE A SERIAL KILLER OR ONE OF THOSE PEOPLE WHO KEEP TRYING TO START "THE WAVE" WHEN NO ONE AROUND YOU IS INTERESTED, **THERE IS NOTHING WRONG WITH YOU**.

—YOU DO YOU

Stop freaking out about shit
you can't control.

AND

Enable yourself to make
rational decisions.

SO YOU CAN

Solve problems instead
of making them worse.

—CALM THE FUCK DOWN

IT'S OKAY TO SAY NO

WHENEVER YOU GODDAMN PLEASE,

TO WHOMEVER YOU GODDAMN MUST,

AND YOU DON'T HAVE TO BE SO

GODDAMN SORRY ABOUT IT.

—FUCK NO!

THE
NOTSORRY
METHOD

STEP 1:

DECIDE what you don't
give a fuck about

STEP 2:

DON'T give a fuck
about those things

Deciding you don't give a fuck about something is extremely liberating. Not giving that fuck—and doing so without hurting other people's feelings or being an asshole—is even better. The goal of the NotSorry Method is to pare away the fucks that don't bring you joy, *paving* the way for the fucks that do. If you follow it, your spirit will be lighter, your calendar clearer, and your time and energy spent on only the things and people you truly enjoy.

—THE LIFE-CHANGING MAGIC OF NOT GIVING A FUCK

Saying no is about setting and protecting all kinds of **boundaries**— even when you technically *can* say yes, but you *shouldn't*. Or frankly, you could, but you *just don't want to.*

—FUCK NO!

Once you
FACE REALITY,
you can start bending it
TO YOUR WILL.

—GET YOUR SHIT TOGETHER

IT IS ABSOLUTELY OKAY—AND
HEALTHY—TO BE CONCERNED WITH
YOUR OWN SELF-INTEREST, WHICH
YOU CAN DO WHILE *ALSO* LOOKING
OUT FOR OTHERS. BEING **SELFISH**
AND BEING **SELFLESS** DON'T HAVE
TO BE MUTUALLY EXCLUSIVE.

—YOU DO YOU

selfish

(adj.) [pronounced self-ISH]:

Looking out for yourself while also not being an asshole, an insufferable prick, or a psychopath.

When shit happens, circumstances are what they are: tires are flat, wrists are broken, files are deleted, hamsters are dead. **The only thing you can control is YOU, and your reaction.**

—CALM THE FUCK DOWN

You do not have to say yes

to free shit just because someone wants to give it to you. All you have to say is "I wouldn't have anywhere to hang a ten-foot-long latch hook version of *The Last Supper,* but thanks!"

—FUCK NO!

INSTEAD OF
TRYING TO
CHANGE YOU,
**LET'S CELEBRATE
WHAT IT MEANS
TO *BE* YOU**—
IN ALL YOUR
WEIRD, DIFFICULT,
SELFISH, IMPERFECT,
ANTISOCIAL,
OVEREXCITED,
UNIQUE, AND
UNCONVENTIONAL
WAYS.

—YOU DO YOU

The day I stopped giving a fuck about
how I looked in a bathing suit,
it was like a litter of kittens in black leotards had tumbled
down from heaven to perform "All the Single Ladies" for
the sole enjoyment of my thighs and belly.

—THE LIFE-CHANGING MAGIC OF NOT GIVING A FUCK

*Change doesn't
start with cleaning out
the garage. It starts with*

CLEANING OUT
YOUR MIND.

—GET YOUR SHIT TOGETHER

ARE YOU WORRIED THAT YOUR
FRIENDS WILL BE MAD AT YOU IF
YOU TELL THEM THE POLITE TRUTH?
THEN YOU WORRY TOO MUCH.

—THE LIFE-CHANGING MAGIC OF NOT GIVING A FUCK

FREAKING OUT
IS NOT GOING TO SOLVE YOUR PROBLEM.

—CALM THE FUCK DOWN

No is an option. And it isn't just for RSVP cards. It's for colleagues who ask you to cover for them for the third time this week and second cousins seeking interest-free loans. It's for bosses who want you to work too much and clients who want to pay too little. It's for kids and dates and roommates and phone solicitors and third tequila shots.

No is an acceptable answer.

It's time to start using it.

—FUCK NO!

NOT GIVING A FUCK begins with taking inventory of your mental space so you can sort all of the fucks being demanded of you into **those that bring JOY** and **those that ANNOY**. Then you can decide to give (or not give) them accordingly.

—THE LIFE-CHANGING MAGIC OF NOT GIVING A FUCK

On Mental Decluttering

Imagine your mind is a barn.

It contains all of the stuff you're being
asked to give a fuck about right now,
whether you *want to* or *have to*, or not.

That barn is a big fucking mess.

TIME TO CLEAN IT OUT.

LIFE IS LIKE AN ADULT COLORING BOOK.

YOU SIMPLY WORK YOUR WAY THROUGH EACH LITTLE SECTION UNTIL THE BIG PICTURE MATERIALIZES BEFORE YOU.

—GET YOUR SHIT TOGETHER

There is nothing wrong with liking things the way you like them and asking for what you want. There is also nothing wrong with aggressively pursuing what you want when it lies outside the bounds of what other people approve of or feel like dealing with.

You probably shouldn't go all Meg Ryan *every* time you go out to dinner (unless you really enjoy the flavor profile of someone else's saliva added to your halibut), but you also don't have to constantly settle for less than you want, need, or deserve.

—YOU DO YOU

fucksorcism *(n)*:

An exorcism of the fucks you no longer want to give.

Not giving a fuck means
allowing yourself to say *No*.

I DON'T WANT TO. I DON'T HAVE TIME.
I CAN'T AFFORD IT.

Not giving a fuck means releasing
yourself from the worry, anxiety, fear, and
guilt associated with saying no.

Not giving a fuck means eliminating annoying
stuff from your life, freeing up space to enjoy all of
the stuff you DO give a fuck about.
It's that simple.

—THE LIFE-CHANGING MAGIC OF NOT GIVING A FUCK

THE ONE QUESTION
TO RULE THEM ALL

CAN I CONTROL IT?

Asking "Can I control it?" is the standard by which you measure whether something is worth your worries—and what, if anything, you can do about it.

If you can accept that the sky is blue and water is wet and macarons are disappointing and borderline fraudulent as a dessert,

you can accept the things you can't control.

You don't have to like it; you just have to accept the reality of the situation.

—CALM THE FUCK DOWN

Being "difficult" means being confident and vocal, challenging yourself and others, and **standing up for what you believe in**—even if that *also* means taking an unpopular stance or forging an unusual path.

—YOU DO YOU

You do not have to say yes
all the time JUST BECAUSE *you've*
said it a few times before.

—FUCK NO!

On making a Fuck Budget

Your "fuck bucks" = time, energy, and/or money spent on giving a fuck. These resources are limited, so **giving a fuck to something means one *less* fuck you have to spend on something else**.

Too often, we allocate our fucks without an end goal in sight. In order to maximize your potential for happiness, you need to consider outcomes *before* saying yes to people, tasks, obligations, and events. **Stop. Calculate. And maybe don't give that fuck?**

—THE LIFE-CHANGING MAGIC OF NOT GIVING A FUCK

The biggest obstacle to "doing you" is doing things *just because* that's how everyone else does them, or because it's the way those things have always been done.
Down with the Tyranny of Just Because!

—YOU DO YOU

GET
YOUR
SHIT
TOGETHER

AND
START
WINNING AT
LIFE!

CONFERENCE CALLS ARE THE PERFECT STORM OF NONPRODUCTIVITY: AN EXCUSE TO GET ABSOLUTELY NOTHING ACCOMPLISHED AND WASTE LITERALLY EVERYONE'S TIME. **STOP GIVING A FUCK ABOUT CONFERENCE CALLS,** AND GAIN THREE OR FOUR UNENCUMBERED HOURS PER WEEK IN WHICH YOU CAN GET ACTUAL WORK DONE.

—THE LIFE-CHANGING MAGIC OF NOT GIVING A FUCK

Much has been written by more science-y people than me about **the myth of multitasking**, but suffice it to say, it's not actually possible to do more than one thing at a time. And if you're trying to do multiple things at once, I can guarantee you're not doing any of them *well*.

—GET YOUR SHIT TOGETHER

WHEN SHIT HITS THE FAN,

you'll wish you'd spent less energy freaking out about it and had more left in the tank to devote to

DEALING WITH IT.

—CALM THE FUCK DOWN

A FUCK
NOT GIVEN
IS SOMETHING
GAINED.

—THE LIFE-CHANGING MAGIC OF NOT GIVING A FUCK

When it comes to a to-do list,
writing one down is only half the battle.

Next, you have to whittle it down,
according to what you need to do first
and what can be pushed off until later.

PRIORITIZE!

—GET YOUR SHIT TOGETHER

THE
MUST-DO
METHOD

1. **MAKE** a to-do list

2. **PRIORITIZE** items based on *urgency*

3. **MOVE** what has to get done **TODAY** to a must-do list

4. **DO** that stuff and save the rest for tomorrow

5. **REPEAT** steps 1–4

STOP LETTING OTHER
PEOPLE TELL YOU WHAT TO DO,
HOW TO DO IT, OR WHY IT
CAN'T BE DONE.

—YOU DO YOU

An informed citizen doesn't have to gather information over breakfast, on the toilet, astride an exercise bike, AND right before bed. A once-daily news dump is sufficient to **keep you in the know** without also keeping your blood pressure higher than Snoop Dogg.

—CALM THE FUCK DOWN

NO.
One word,
complete sentence.
No muss, no fuss.

—FUCK NO!

Time is your best friend and worst enemy. It is the mother ship from which two competing forces—prioritization and procrastination—descend to create order or wreak chaos on your life. Once you understand how time applies to your life, you'll be able to use it as a force for good instead of a force for missing flights or pissing off your dinner date.

—GET YOUR SHIT TOGETHER

Stand up for yourself—and for other people. **Having the courage of your convictions isn't being "difficult." It's** admirable, and it will also get you a better table.

—YOU DO YOU

Don't give a fuck about your Facebook friend's constant drama? **"SNOOZE FOR 30 DAYS"** *is one of the easiest ways to not give a fuck ever invented. None of the confrontation of "Unfriend" and all of the benefits!*

—THE LIFE-CHANGING MAGIC OF NOT GIVING A FUCK

Saying no will help you delegate more and panic less. It will help you focus *better* on *fewer* things, setting yourself up for success at what's most important to you. It will help you stop giving inches and save you many, many miles. And it will help you **let go of expectations**—*for* yourself and *of* others—that don't serve you.

—FUCK NO!

Prioritizing is magical. Like playing the kazoo, it's really not that hard, it makes you feel good, and **anyone can do it.**

—GET YOUR SHIT TOGETHER

You can't please everyone, so you've got to please yourself. Ricky Nelson sang it all the way to the Top 40 back in 1972 and **GIRL WAS NOT WRONG.**

—YOU DO YOU

50

STOP SPENDING TIME YOU DON'T HAVE WITH PEOPLE YOU DON'T LIKE DOING THINGS **YOU DON'T WANT TO DO.**

—THE LIFE-CHANGING MAGIC OF NOT GIVING A FUCK

STAKING OUT YOUR
TERRITORY LOUD AND CLEAR
WORKS FOR THE MONGOOSE
AND IT CAN WORK FOR YOU.

BOUNDARIES, BABY!

—FUCK NO!

PRACTICE YOUR ABC'S:

Acceptance Breeds Confidence.

—YOU DO YOU

THE
NOWORRIES
METHOD

STEP 1:

CALM the fuck down

STEP 2:

DEAL with it

How much time do you spend worrying about something that hasn't happened yet? Or about something that not only hasn't happened, but probably won't? And how many hours have you wasted freaking out about something that has already happened, instead of just, you know, dealing with it?

—CALM THE FUCK DOWN

Everything is easier if you break it down into SMALL, MANAGEABLE CHUNKS.

Living your life according to other people's definitions of success is the same as living your life according to other people's dreams, other people's fears, and other people's notions of risk and regret. That's not helping anybody. And the only person it hurts when you shape your life according to other people's standards?

YOU.

—YOU DO YOU

When you learn how to say no and stick to it, it's a positive development for everyone. This is the **JOY OF NO**—and as with cooking and sex, there are plenty of recipes and positions to get you there.

—FUCK NO!

THE **NUMBER OF FUCKS** YOU PERSONALLY HAVE TO GIVE IS A FINITE AND PRECIOUS COMMODITY.

—THE LIFE-CHANGING MAGIC OF NOT GIVING A FUCK

CONFIDENCE is the greatest strength you can cultivate. Your ego is where your confidence lies; ideally, it would be as capacious as an Olympic swimming pool and its contents as robust as the forearms on a Swedish lumberjack.

—YOU DO YOU

fuck overload (n):

The state resulting from having given too many fucks—without enough time, energy, or money to devote to them.

You're overbooked, overwhelmed, and overdrawn.

You have to lobby for your hobby.
Ensure that pleasure activities
are well represented on your calendar
by *scheduling them in*.

—GET YOUR SHIT TOGETHER

Stop dwelling on unlikely outcomes in favor of acting to create more likely ones. Plow forward rather than agonizing backward. Separate your anxiety about what might occur from the act of handling it when it *does* occur.

—CALM THE FUCK DOWN

Family:

If you prick them, do they not bleed? If you tickle them, do they not laugh? And if you politely decline to attend your cousin's wedding, did they not literally give you the option to say no right there on the RSVP card?

—FUCK NO!

Brings joy? By all means,
keep giving a fuck!

But does it *ANNOY*?

Then you need to
STOP GIVING A FUCK,
posthaste.

Failure is just a thing that happens. Sometimes you bring it on yourself, like when you go to Burning Man without adequate sunscreen and Wet Wipes. **Get your shit together and deal with it.**

—GET YOUR SHIT TOGETHER

ALL OF THE QUALITIES—YES,
EVEN THE FLAWS—THAT MAKE YOU,
YOU, ALSO MAKE YOU **INTERESTING,**
CAPABLE, AND **POWERFUL** IN
YOUR OWN WAY.

—YOU DO YOU

Think of your time, energy, and money
like three prized sheep—easy prey for clever thieves
and ravenous wolves, unless you, their shepherd,
set some boundaries to **protect them.**

—FUCK NO!

PROVEN FACT:
You cannot finish something you never start.

—GET YOUR SHIT TOGETHER

Show me someone who's planned a big event and hasn't been plagued by **what-ifs and worries** and I'll show you a superhuman who runs on Klonopin and hubris.

—CALM THE FUCK DOWN

Accept yourself before you wreck yourself.

—YOU DO YOU

ARE YOU STRESSED OUT,
OVERBOOKED, AND/OR
UNDERWHELMED BY LIFE?

IF THE ANSWER IS YES, YOU MAY
BE GIVING **TOO MANY FUCKS.**

—THE LIFE-CHANGING MAGIC OF NOT GIVING A FUCK

"**Get your
shit together**"
is not an admonition.

IT'S A **RALLYING CRY**.

—GET YOUR SHIT TOGETHER

When shit happens, you gotta be flexible.

Remember: if you're still bending, you're not broken.

—CALM THE FUCK DOWN

BE THE *SANTA OF FUCKS!*

Instead of toys, you're walking around with a bag
of fucks and only doling them out to the boys
and girls you deem worthy.

—THE LIFE-CHANGING MAGIC OF NOT GIVING A FUCK

When someone asks if they can bring a plus-one to your wedding or take your window seat, they are asking because they know full well that it is not automatically okay to just do those things.

Askers gonna ask.

You're allowed to say no.

—FUCK NO!

If you're adept at imagining the worst
before it even happens, you can
apply that same obsessive creativity
to dealing with it when it does!

Turn your *WHAT-IFS*
into *NOW-WHATS*
and make a plan of attack.

—CALM THE FUCK DOWN

IT'S ONE THING TO HAVE
AN *OH SHIT* MOMENT, BUT IT'S
QUITE ANOTHER TO ACTUALLY
DO SOMETHING ABOUT IT.

—GET YOUR SHIT TOGETHER

Un-dealt-with shit begets more shit.
Like, refusing to tend to that pesky wound you got
while chopping down your Christmas tree may
mean spending the New Year learning to operate
a prosthetic hand better than you operate an axe.

When in doubt, *DEAL WITH YOUR SHIT.*

—CALM THE FUCK DOWN

IF YOU'RE

NOT DOING

YOU,

YOU'RE SCREWING YOU.

ON SAYING HONEST, POLITE NO'S

Instead of hemming, hawing, and leaving people hanging, you'll be letting them down quickly and gently. They'll appreciate it! Wouldn't you?

Instead of doing things with and for your family under duress, stoking the fires of resentment and creating the wrong kind of memories, you'll be preserving the quality of the time you *do* spend together.

Instead of overcommitting and potentially under-delivering, you'll be setting manageable expectations that prevent coworkers from getting burned when your circuits overload.

—FUCK NO!

Not giving a fuck means TAKING CARE OF YOURSELF FIRST— *like affixing your own oxygen mask before helping others.*

—THE LIFE-CHANGING MAGIC OF NOT GIVING A FUCK

There's so much more you *could* be doing
with your life, if you can just stop worrying about
what you *should* be doing.

—GET YOUR SHIT TOGETHER

THERE SHOULDN'T BE ANY STIGMA ATTACHED
TO THERAPY, MEDICATION, AND GETTING HELP.
MENTAL HEALTH IS JUST AS IMPORTANT
AS PHYSICAL HEALTH, AND IF TENDING TO
YOURS MEANS BEING OPEN ABOUT ITS CARE
AND FEEDING, GO NUTS.

—YOU DO YOU

Before you can **attack your anxiety** *about* a problem, you must identify the problem itself. One at a time, please.

—CALM THE FUCK DOWN

Family—and all its group photos, weddings, bar and bat mitzvahs, christenings, quinceañeras, all-inclusive vacations, group-therapy sessions, right-wing uncles, sibling rivalries, drama, and grudges—promotes constant, daily fuck-giving.

—THE LIFE-CHANGING MAGIC OF NOT GIVING A FUCK

Needing or *wanting to give a fuck*
about something is not the same as actually
being able to do it. For that, you also
have to get your shit together.

—GET YOUR SHIT TOGETHER

3 STEPS
FOR GETTING
YOUR SHIT TOGETHER

STRATEGIZE:

Set a goal and make a plan
to achieve that goal in a series
of small, manageable chunks.

FOCUS:

Set aside time to
complete each chunk.

COMMIT:

Do what you need to do
to check off your chunks!

SHINE ON, YOU CRAZY DIAMONDS.

—YOU DO YOU

Stop thinking about saying *no* as too hard, wicked rude, and just plain unacceptable, and start thinking about it as pretty easy, perfectly polite, and eminently justifiable, actually.

—FUCK NO!

FREAKOUT FUNDS =

TIME, ENERGY, AND MONEY

Looking at problems rationally and based on all available data helps you **BUDGET YOUR FREAKOUT FUNDS** effectively. You could spend them exacerbating your freakout, or you could spend them calming the fuck down and dealing with the shit that caused it. Up to you.

—CALM THE FUCK DOWN

BELIEVING THAT YOU HAVE ANY CONTROL OVER WHAT OTHER PEOPLE THINK—AND WASTING YOUR FUCKS ON THAT PURSUIT—IS FUTILE. IT IS A RECIPE FOR FAILURE ON A GRAND FUCKING SCALE.

—THE LIFE-CHANGING MAGIC OF NOT GIVING A FUCK

You're the boss.
You are the **Tony Danza**
of your mind.*

—GET YOUR SHIT TOGETHER

* Or the Judith Light? I'm not actually sure which one of them was the boss.

**ACCEPT
YOUR
BODY**
FOR
WHAT
IT IS
RATHER
THAN
PUNISHING
IT FOR
WHAT IT
ISN'T.

—YOU DO YOU

If something is highly unlikely to happen, *why are you worrying about it?* And if it's far off in the distance, why are you worrying about it NOW?

—CALM THE FUCK DOWN

We need to get comfortable **saying no for our own health**—and the health of our relationships with family, friends, lovers, bosses, colleagues, clients, roommates, teammates, and everyone else who needs to hear it.

—FUCK NO!

When you start giving fewer, better fucks, you'll be **happier** at work and your colleagues and clients will benefit. You'll be **better rested** and **more fun** around friends. You might spend more time with your family—or you might spend less, making those moments you do share all the more precious.

—THE LIFE-CHANGING MAGIC OF NOT GIVING A FUCK

The only people who do not need calendars are drifters and deities. The former don't have anywhere to be and the latter are omnipresent. You?

You need a calendar.

—GET YOUR SHIT TOGETHER

IF YOU'RE CONSIDERED THE "BLACK SHEEP" OF YOUR FAMILY, IT MAY SIMPLY BE THAT YOU DON'T LIKE THE SAME THINGS YOUR SIBLINGS LIKE OR VALUE THE SAME THINGS YOUR PARENTS VALUE.

SO. FUCKING. WHAT.

—YOU DO YOU

It's not the rest of the world's job to DEAL WITH YOUR SHIT.

—CALM THE FUCK DOWN

Life is a series of yes-or-no choices,
fucks given and fucks withheld.
It's time to stop giving all of
YOUR fucks to all the wrong things
for all the wrong reasons.

—THE LIFE-CHANGING MAGIC OF NOT GIVING A FUCK

A PITY PARTY IS A SHITTY PARTY.

—GET YOUR SHIT TOGETHER

Make it a habit to reward yourself for good behavior—because if you're always waiting around for other people to pat you on the back, you're likely to wind up standing in the middle of the room for a long time looking like a dumbass.

—YOU DO YOU

YOU MAY THINK

I can't possibly stop giving
a fuck about what other people think.

IT'S IN MY DNA!

But in order to live your best life,
you're going to have to

HACK THE SYSTEM.

—THE LIFE-CHANGING MAGIC OF NOT GIVING A FUCK

IT'S TRUE THAT "THERE AREN'T
ENOUGH HOURS IN THE DAY"
TO DO EVERYTHING.

**BUT YOU DON'T HAVE
TO DO EVERYTHING**.

YOU ONLY HAVE TO DO
THE THINGS THAT YOU
PRIORITIZED.

BOOM.

—GET YOUR SHIT TOGETHER

IF YOU FREAK OUT ALL THE TIME
ABOUT EVERYTHING, YOU SPEND HEAVILY
AGAINST YOUR ACCOUNT OF GOODWILL.
YOU'RE IN DANGER OF OVERDRAWING IT FASTER
THAN THEY DRAIN THE AQUARIUM AFTER
A KID FALLS INTO THE SHARK TANK.

—CALM THE FUCK DOWN

WHEN THE GOING GETS TOUGH,
having the courage of your convictions is admirable—
especially when you have better things to be doing than
defending your needs, desires, and values to a bunch
of people who don't understand why you care so deeply
about something they don't care about at all.

—YOU DO YOU

Merely thinking about the mayhem you *could* visit upon your enemies is a **terrific mood booster**. Though "accidentally" upending a bottle of clam juice into Carl's open car window on your way to work is fun too.

—CALM THE FUCK DOWN

Fuckscapade *(n)*:

An event to which you gave more fucks than
you should have.

THE LIFE-CHANGING MAGIC OF
NOT GIVING A FUCK IS ALL ABOUT
PRIORITIZING. JOY OVER ANNOY.
CHOICE OVER OBLIGATION.
STICK TO YOUR FUCK BUDGET.
EYES ON THE PRIZE.

—THE LIFE-CHANGING MAGIC OF NOT GIVING A FUCK

Humans discovered fire,
mapped the Arctic Circle,
and created hologram Tupac.
**We didn't do any of that
shit without a plan!**

—GET YOUR SHIT TOGETHER

IF YOU'RE SERIOUS ABOUT
GETTING YOUR SHIT TOGETHER
IN THE LONG TERM, YOU HAVE TO
STRATEGIZE, FOCUS, AND COMMIT
IN THE SHORT TERM. SPEND THE TIME
NOW TO SAVE IT LATER.

—GET YOUR SHIT TOGETHER

THE FRIENDS
WHO DON'T JUDGE YOU

for choosing what's best for you

are the ones you'll want to keep

closer than anyone.

—YOU DO YOU

Avoidance is the difference between napping as healthy self-care and napping as unhealthy coping mechanism. Don't ruin napping for yourself.

JUST STOP AVOIDING YOUR SHIT.

—CALM THE FUCK DOWN

YOUR LIFE CAN BE SO MUCH BETTER WHEN YOU **LEARN TO SAY NO** WITH CONFIDENCE—AND WITHOUT GUILT, STIGMA, FEAR, AND REGRET.

—FUCK NO!

When the **Zombie Apocalypse** comes,
focus group mentality will
be the death of us all.

—YOU DO YOU

It is a truth universally acknowledged that family members tend to think other family members have to give a fuck about their lives just because they share DNA. Think about that for a hot second. **Does it make any sense at all? No, it does not.**

—THE LIFE-CHANGING MAGIC OF NOT GIVING A FUCK

RELATIONSHIPS NEED TIME
AND ENERGY IN ORDER TO
THRIVE—THIS IS NOT
A PACKAGE OF SEA MONKEYS
YOU'RE RAISING IN
AN OLD MAYONNAISE JAR.

—GET YOUR SHIT TOGETHER

IT'S NO USE KNOWING **HOW** TO SAY NO IF YOU DON'T KNOW **WHEN** TO SAY NO. YOU NEED TO SET SOME BOUNDARIES.

—FUCK NO!

YOU MIGHT
DIE TOMORROW.
BE SELFISH TODAY.

—YOU DO YOU

*Most people do not
care nearly as much about*
HOW YOU LIVE YOUR LIFE
as you think they do.

—FUCK NO!

If you decide you don't give a fuck about the company picnic, just . . . don't go. You don't have to call in a bomb threat to get it canceled—just offer your regrets in a timely fashion.

Honestly?

Nobody cares if you're there anyway. You're kind of standoffish.

—THE LIFE-CHANGING MAGIC OF NOT GIVING A FUCK

GETTING YOUR SHIT
TOGETHER FOR **THE BIG STUFF**
IS JUST GETTING YOUR SHIT
TOGETHER FOR A **BUNCH
OF SMALL STUFF,** OVER TIME.

—GET YOUR SHIT TOGETHER

IF YOUR STARRING ROLE ON EARTH IS A LIMITED RUN—AND I HATE TO BREAK IT TO YOU, BUT IT SURELY IS—**WHY IMPOSE LIMITS ON THE HAPPINESS** YOU CAN HAVE WHILE YOU'RE STILL HERE?

—YOU DO YOU

GUILT IS NOT A HAPPY FEELING.

It's more like that feeling when you have a sudden, agonizing itch in your crotch area but you're surrounded by people and you can't dig in after it and you're *dying* to get some relief. That is what guilt feels like.

Not giving a fuck should always result in greater pleasure, satisfaction, and happiness. **Not crotch itch.**

—THE LIFE-CHANGING MAGIC OF NOT GIVING A FUCK

GOOD THINGS

COME TO THOSE WHO DELEGATE.

—GET YOUR SHIT TOGETHER

Channel your anger into something productive. For example, after hurling every glass container in your home against a wall as though it were an old white man trying to steal your children's future, take out the recycling.

Smash the patriarchy, save the planet!

—CALM THE FUCK DOWN

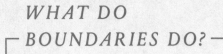

WHAT DO
BOUNDARIES DO?

They protect things!

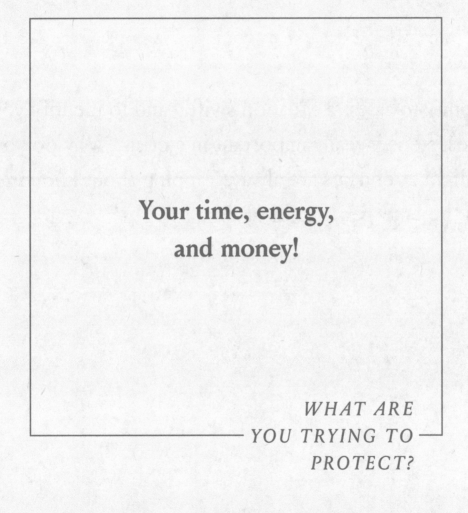

Your time, energy,
and money!

*WHAT ARE
YOU TRYING TO
PROTECT?*

The ability to assess a situation swiftly and to identify your next best steps is really important in a crisis. Why do you think flight attendants are always yapping about **knowing where the emergency exits are?**

—CALM THE FUCK DOWN

DON'T BE A HERO.

Give yourself the time and space
to do the shit that needs doing,
to get you closer to your goal.

—GET YOUR SHIT TOGETHER

Being concerned about yourself doesn't exclude you from also being *generous, caring, attentive, and empathetic* toward others. It might even be what enables you to BE those things.

—YOU DO YOU

FAMILY IS A FUCKING MINEFIELD

—THE LIFE-CHANGING MAGIC OF NOT GIVING A FUCK

BE THE NO
YOU WANT TO HEAR
IN THE WORLD!

—FUCK NO!

Many of us are locked into a *Groundhog Day*-style malaise when it comes to outdated rituals related to holidays, vacations, and other family gatherings. Thanksgiving might as well be renamed **"Fucksgiving."** Religious holidays like Christmas, Easter, and Hanukkah are double the dogma, double the fucks.

Well guess what?

Just because this is how your family has always done something doesn't mean this is how you have to do it until the end of time.

—THE LIFE-CHANGING MAGIC OF NOT GIVING A FUCK

Staring blankly at your to-do list does not cause the items on it to migrate dutifully off the page like **a herd of goddamn lemmings.**

—GET YOUR SHIT TOGETHER

RULES COME IN ALL SHAPES AND SIZES.

Spoken rules, unspoken rules, passive-aggressive signage at the public pool. Some of them are there for good reason, but many are not as useful as you've been led to believe.

If it's hurting or limiting you *more* than it's helping others, it might be **a rule worth breaking.**

—YOU DO YOU

Focus on the reality of your situation instead of **obsessing over what-ifs** that are as unrealistic as the "after" photos in an ad for cut-rate diet pills. We all know she just went for a spray tan, sucked in her stomach, and **tricked out the tatas** in a more flattering bra.

—CALM THE FUCK DOWN

IF SOMEONE REFUSES TO TAKE YOUR NO FOR AN ANSWER, PERHAPS **THAT SAYS MORE ABOUT THEM** THAN IT DOES ABOUT YOU.

—FUCK NO!

You get back so much TIME when you put your fucks in order. Time to meditate quietly on the toilet instead of rushing to get on a conference call; time to cultivate that prizewinning fudge recipe instead of reading *Moby-Dick* for book club; time to spend with loved ones instead of, well, time to spend with some random fuckers you don't even like.

—THE LIFE-CHANGING MAGIC OF NOT GIVING A FUCK

The best, most potentially winning path toward achieving your creative goals lies between **finding time** *and* granting yourself **permission to use it**.

—GET YOUR SHIT TOGETHER

At the end of the day,
we all have our shit.

We all have our hang-ups,
everybody's different,
and then everybody dies.

In the meantime,
why not live your best life?

—YOU DO YOU

Guilt is the most powerful
motivator for doing things we can't,
shouldn't, or don't want to do.

I want you to lower
your hackles, open your arms,

and *RELEASE THAT
GUILT INTO THE AIR*

like a sack of motherfucking doves.

—FUCK NO!

CALM
THE FUCK
DOWN

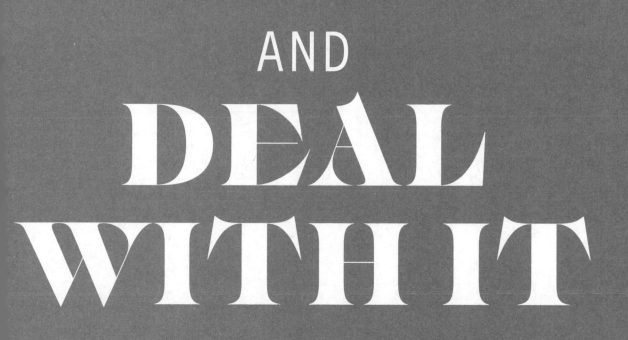

AND
DEAL
WITH IT

Apologizing is like lube.
Not strictly necessary, but it reduces
friction and makes things easier and
more pleasant for both parties.

—FUCK NO!

Wear a gimp suit and sequined heels
to your performance evaluation and immediately
become **the mayor of No Fucks Given.**

—THE LIFE-CHANGING MAGIC OF NOT GIVING A FUCK

YOUR JOB
IS TO GET
YOUR SHIT
TOGETHER,
NOT WORRY
ABOUT
EVERYONE
ELSE'S.

—GET YOUR SHIT TOGETHER

If you "selfishly" take a corner piece from the brownie pan, you're showing at least three other people it's okay to take one too. **Lead by example, friend.**

Control what you can
and accept what you can't
so you can stop freaking out
and get on with your life.

—CALM THE FUCK DOWN

A donut cannot force you to eat it. You have all the power in this relationship.

A presentation does not demand that you re-jigger every slide in a slightly more attractive font. You decide if that is truly a good use of your time.

A restaurant will not fail because you didn't have the time, energy, or wherewithal to eat a ludicrously priced ramekin of celery foam this weekend.

—FUCK NO!

The power of honesty cannot be overstated.
I can't tell you how many *MORE* fucks you wind up
giving when you beat around the bush.

God, even that expression sounds exhausting.

—THE LIFE-CHANGING MAGIC OF NOT GIVING A FUCK

IT'S PERFECTLY NATURAL FOR SOME FRIENDSHIPS
TO FALL BY THE WAYSIDE, AT ANY STAGE OF LIFE.
THE CHALLENGE IS MAINTAINING OR IMPROVING
THE ONES THAT ARE REALLY IMPORTANT TO YOU.

—GET YOUR SHIT TOGETHER

Don't be shy about
GETTING THE BEST DEAL
for yourself that you can.

—YOU DO YOU

WHEN SHIT HAPPENS, YOU NEED TO **ACKNOWLEDGE** IT, **ACCEPT** THE PARTS YOU CAN'T CONTROL, AND THEN **ADDRESS** THE PARTS YOU CAN.

—CALM THE FUCK DOWN

Thinking about
the consequences of
saying yes will help you take
the action of saying no.

—FUCK NO!

There will be many items added to your Fuck Budget when you inherit a bunch of in-laws. But if you think about it—they inherited you too. And *your* religious values, *your* political views, and *your* aversion to dressing in matching turtlenecks for group photos. When it comes to not giving a fuck, **you might have more in common than you realize**.

—THE LIFE-CHANGING MAGIC OF NOT GIVING A FUCK

Getting your shit together isn't all email and piggy banks; you also need to go to the doctor and renew your passport and learn to dispatch annoying chores with skill and vigor. **Stop paying late fees and start writing thank-you notes!**

—GET YOUR SHIT TOGETHER

In order to feel comfortable making decisions in the first place, **you have to feel comfortable getting a few of them wrong**. Because you WILL get a few of them wrong. And when you do, you can't let yourself be permanently sidelined by regret.

—YOU DO YOU

GETTING ANGRY
MAKES THINGS WORSE.

—CALM THE FUCK DOWN

"I'll have to think about that" is a polite, natural way **to press pause on the conversation** until you're ready to resume— be that in two minutes, two days, or two weeks from never.

—FUCK NO!

If you find certain meetings to be black holes of useless chatter, not to mention **a total waste of your time**, then you may have to attend them, but you could stop giving a fuck about *paying attention*. And you can most certainly stop giving a fuck about *taking notes*. Seriously, have you ever used the notes you took in a meeting? Let's be real.

—THE LIFE-CHANGING MAGIC OF NOT GIVING A FUCK

WHERE DO I BEGIN?

That's easy. You begin by

SETTING A GOAL.

—GET YOUR SHIT TOGETHER

LEARN HOW TO TAKE **A FUCKING COMPLIMENT** EVERY ONCE IN A WHILE.

—YOU DO YOU

Sad? Treat yourself the way you would treat a sad friend in need. Be kind. Naps, chocolate, a *Broad City* marathon; whatever relieves your funk or puts a spring back in your step and a giggle in your wiggle.

—CALM THE FUCK DOWN

STOP
SAYING
YES

WHEN YOU
WANT TO SAY
FUCK NO!

If you're someone who says "I'm always spending a little bit more than I should" and going into debt, then you're allowing money to build a prison around you and make you its bitch.

Don't be money's bitch.

—GET YOUR SHIT TOGETHER

LET THAT TIGER OUT
OF THE CAGE AND GET
THOSE **FREAK FLAGS**
RIPPLING ON THE BREEZE!

—YOU DO YOU

If you can't opt out of the group
family photo, wear your kinkiest or most hilarious
undergarments on that day, and then every time your
mother shares the pic on Facebook you'll take secret
pleasure in knowing you were wearing your
POISON PARTIED HERE thong.

—THE LIFE-CHANGING MAGIC OF NOT GIVING A FUCK

TIME, LIKE
irritable bowel syndrome,
CAN BE MANAGED.

—GET YOUR SHIT TOGETHER

In the immortal words of
Destiny's Child . . . **are you ready for this?**

THERE IS NOTHING WRONG WITH YOU.

—YOU DO YOU

IN THE AGE OF SMARTPHONE
CAMERAS, EVERY MELTDOWN
IS A POTENTIAL FIFTEEN
MINUTES OF INFAMY.

DO YOU WANT TO WIND UP
ON THE EVENING NEWS SPEWING
REGRETTABLE EPITHETS
OR ON FACEBOOK
LIVE DESTROYING PUBLIC
PROPERTY? NO?

THEN CALM THE FUCK DOWN.

—CALM THE FUCK DOWN

Give a man a fish, you feed him for a day.
Teach a man to solve his own fucking problems,
you gain hours of uninterrupted me-time.
It's an ancient Chinese proverb. Look it up.

—FUCK NO!

HOW MUCH BETTER WOULD YOUR LIFE BE IF YOU COULD SAY NO TO THINGS YOU REALLY DON'T GIVE A FUCK ABOUT?

—THE LIFE-CHANGING MAGIC OF NOT GIVING A FUCK

Holding yourself up to an unreasonable standard
is no way to win at life. It's okay to **lower the bar** a tad,
especially when you're just starting out.

—GET YOUR SHIT TOGETHER

WHATEVER SWABS YOUR DECK, SAILOR!

—YOU DO YOU

There may be days when you feel *blah* and *blech* for no reason, and those feelings send you spiraling into the Bad Place.

"No reason," huh?

INCORRECT.

There is a reason for your anxiety, a what-if behind your worry. And if you can name it, you'll be in a much better position to deal with it.

—CALM THE FUCK DOWN

People who are trying to sell you
shit are used to hearing no. They won't
take it personally, and if they do,
they shouldn't be working in sales.

NOT YOUR PROBLEM.

—FUCK NO!

whether you give a fuck (i.e., a care) *about* the matter at hand and whether it deserves a fuck (i.e., your time, energy, or money) *given to* it as a line item on your Fuck Budget.

—THE LIFE-CHANGING MAGIC OF NOT GIVING A FUCK

Do you ever find yourself stuck at the office—or just glued to the couch—when **what you really want** is to go out (for once), get to the gym (at last), or get started on that "someday" project that's been hanging out on your to-do list since, oh, the beginning of time?

Sounds like you need to get your shit together.

—GET YOUR SHIT TOGETHER

ACCEPT
YOURSELF,
THEN
**ACT WITH
CONFIDENCE**.
ACT WITH
CONFIDENCE,
THEN ACCEPT
THE
CONSEQUENCES.

—YOU DO YOU

ALL'S FAIR IN NO AND WAR.

—FUCK NO!

If you have one of those e-calendars that's viewable to everyone in the office, just **start marking entire days "busy"** so nobody can schedule a meeting with you.

No. Fucks. Given.

—THE LIFE-CHANGING MAGIC OF NOT GIVING A FUCK

"Hard" is subjective,
but "too hard" is just another way
of saying "I quit before I even tried."

—GET YOUR SHIT TOGETHER

YOU DON'T
NEED PERMISSION
TO BE YOURSELF,

MAKE YOUR
OWN DECISIONS
AND MISTAKES,

**AND REVEL IN YOUR
OWN SUCCESSES**.

—YOU DO YOU

WORRYING IS WASTEFUL.

**IT COSTS YOU TIME,
ENERGY, AND MONEY**

AND GIVES YOU NOTHING
USEFUL IN RETURN.

—CALM THE FUCK DOWN

Being honest helps release you from after-the-fact anxiety associated with saying no. You don't have to worry if people are wondering what the "real" reason is that you're not joining the festivities,

BECAUSE YOU ALREADY TOLD THEM.

—FUCK NO!

THE PATH TO GIVING FEWER, BETTER FUCKS IS PAVED WITH RECLAIMED HOURS, NEWFOUND VERVE, AND COLD HARD CASH.

—THE LIFE-CHANGING MAGIC OF NOT GIVING A FUCK

IN THE GAME OF LIFE, you're competing exclusively against yourself. Not other players, not even the computer. Just you, clearing a path toward victory by **getting your shit together and getting out of your own damn way.**

—GET YOUR SHIT TOGETHER

WHEN SOMEONE TELLS YOU
THAT YOU'D LOOK NICE IF YOU
SMILED MORE, GAZE DIRECTLY
INTO THEIR EYES, UNBLINKING,
UNTIL THEY LOOK AWAY.
THAT'LL TEACH 'EM.

—YOU DO YOU

Standing your ground

after you say no is just

as important and valuable

a lesson as working up

the guts *to* say no.

—FUCK NO!

IF THERE'S A FAMILY HOLIDAY GATHERING YOU JUST CAN'T AVOID, SCHEDULE A MASSAGE FOR THE DAY AFTER SO YOU HAVE SOMETHING TO LOOK FORWARD TO. EVEN BETTER, REQUEST THE MASSAGE AS YOUR HOLIDAY GIFT SO YOUR FAMILY IS ESSENTIALLY **PAYING YOU BACK FOR THE FUCKS YOU GAVE.** IT'S A NEAT TRICK.

—THE LIFE-CHANGING MAGIC OF NOT GIVING A FUCK

The beauty of having your shit together is that **anything is possible.**

"Now isn't a good time for me"
is a terrific all-purpose no.
Honest, polite, and nonspecific:
THE TRIFECTA!

—FUCK NO!

AVOIDANCE
MEANS
NEVER,
EVER
SOLVING
YOUR
PROBLEM.

—CALM THE FUCK DOWN

DON'T SPEND
YOUR TIME AND ENERGY
WORRYING ABOUT
WHAT PEOPLE WILL
THINK ABOUT YOU
"DOING IT YOUR WAY."
JUST DO IT.

—YOU DO YOU

STOP
GIVING
A FUCK

AND START
LIVING
YOUR BEST
LIFE!

ALSO AVAILABLE

the life-changing
magic of NOT GIVING A F*CK

how to stop spending time you don't have
with people you don't like
doing things you don't want to do

A PRACTICAL PARODY

sarah knight

NEW YORK TIMES
BESTSELLER

get
your
SH*T
together

how to stop worrying about what you should do
so you can finish what you need to do
and start doing what you want to do

NEW YORK TIMES bestselling author of
THE LIFE-CHANGING MAGIC OF NOT GIVING A F*CK,
YOU DO YOU, and CALM THE F*CK DOWN

sarah knight

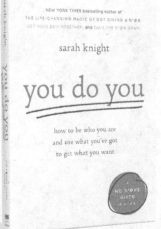

NEW YORK TIMES bestselling author of
THE LIFE-CHANGING MAGIC OF NOT GIVING A F*CK,
GET YOUR SH*T TOGETHER, and CALM THE F*CK DOWN

sarah knight

you do you

how to be who you are
and use what you've got
to get what you want

calm the
F*CK
down

how to control what you can
and accept what you can't
so you can stop freaking out
and get on with your life

sarah knight

NEW YORK TIMES bestselling author of
THE LIFE-CHANGING MAGIC OF NOT GIVING A F*CK,
GET YOUR SH*T TOGETHER, and YOU DO YOU

f*ck no!

how to stop saying yes
when you can't, you shouldn't,
or you just don't want to

sarah knight

NEW YORK TIMES bestselling author of
THE LIFE-CHANGING MAGIC OF NOT GIVING A F*CK,
GET YOUR SH*T TOGETHER, YOU DO YOU,
and CALM THE F*CK DOWN

the life-changing
magic of NOT GIVING A F*CK

JOURNAL

practical ways to care less
and get more

sarah knight

NEW YORK TIMES bestselling author of
GET YOUR SH*T TOGETHER, YOU DO YOU,
CALM THE F*CK DOWN, and F*CK NO!

NEW YORK TIMES bestselling author of
THE LIFE-CHANGING MAGIC OF NOT GIVING A F*CK,
YOU DO YOU, and CALM THE F*CK DOWN

sarah knight

get
your
SH*T
together
JOURNAL

practical ways to cut the bullsh*t and win at life

calm the
F*CK
down

JOURNAL

practical ways to stop worrying
and take control of your life

sarah knight

NEW YORK TIMES bestselling author of
THE LIFE-CHANGING MAGIC OF NOT GIVING A F*CK,
GET YOUR SH*T TOGETHER, YOU DO YOU, and F*CK NO!

PRAISE FOR SARAH KNIGHT

"Genius." —*Cosmopolitan*

"Self-help to swear by." —*Boston Globe*

"Hilarious and truly practical." —*Booklist*

ABOUT THE AUTHOR

Sarah Knight's first book, *The Life-Changing Magic of Not Giving a Fuck,* has been published in more than 30 languages, and her TEDx talk, "The Magic of Not Giving a F*ck," has ten million views. She is a *New York Times* bestselling author whose other titles include *Get Your Shit Together, You Do You, Calm the Fuck Down,* and *Fuck No!* Her writing has appeared in *Glamour, Harper's Bazaar, Marie Claire, Red, Refinery29,* and elsewhere, and she hosts the popular *No F*cks Given* podcast, which hit #1 on the Apple Education charts.

After quitting her corporate job in 2015 to pursue a freelance life, Sarah moved from Brooklyn, New York, to the Dominican Republic, where she currently resides with her husband and two rescue cats, Gladys Knight and Mister Stussy.

You can learn more and sign up for her newsletter at sarahknight.com, and follow Sarah on Instagram, Facebook, and TikTok @sarahknightauthor or on Twitter @MCSnugz.